Managing Modern Security Operations Center & Building Perfect Career as SOC Analyst

Publicancy Ltd

Published by Publicancy Ltd, 2023.

MANAGING MODERN SECURITY OPERATIONS CENTER & BUILDING PERFECT CAREER AS SOC ANALYST

First edition. July 18, 2023.

Copyright © 2023 Publicancy Ltd.

ISBN: 979-8223842675

Written by Publicancy Ltd.

Managing
Modern Security
Operations
Center & Building
Perfect Career As SOC Analyst

A Comprehensive Guide to Security Systems & Various Methods for SOC

Copyright © 2023 by Publicancy Ltd

First Printing, 2023

Chapter 1: Security Operations and Management

Information security is a set of practices intended to keep information secure from unauthorized access or alterations. No doubt, information and data are the most valuable and critical assets for any organization. It is no surprise that information security is becoming the most primary concern for businesses of all nature. There are several active and passive security solutions available depending on the industry and size of business. Organizations not only need to implement solutions but also need to implement a strategy that will keep businesses ahead of the growing security threats.

The CIA Triad

There are three main principles of information security i.e. confidentiality, integrity and availability.

Confidentiality

By definition, confidentiality means to not disclose sensitive information to unauthorized entities. This is one of the most critical, and primary principle of information security. Every organization, whether it belongs to government, politics, industries, education, or health need to keep their data confidential. There is always some confidential information and data which needs to be secret among stakeholders, data owners, and other authorized entities. For example, a password is a type of information which always needs to remain confidential.

Integrity

Integrity is another important property of information or data which has not been altered in an unauthorized manner since it was created, transmitted, or stored. In any business, information needs to be shared, processed, and passed among different people. It is necessary to maintain the integrity of information throughout every process. For example, if a person sends information to another person, it is necessary that the information is received as it is without any modifications. If any modifications are required, they should be carried out by authorized personals only.

Availability

Availability is the third property of CIA triad. It means information, data, and services are always available to be accessed by users. An organization may suffer a great loss if its availability is compromised.

Security operations are a set of activities that help to maintain the ongoing security posture of an organization. Security Operations (in SOC) include monitoring, detecting, investigating, responding, and reporting security events. These are continuous operations running all the time throughout the year. However, before starting these security operations, an organization goes through planning and implementation phases.

Introduction to Security Operation Center

Security Operation Center (SOC), as the name suggests, is a central operation center which deals with information and cyber security events by employing people, processes, and technology. It continuously monitors and improves an organization's security posture. It is considered as the first line of defense against cyber security threats.

SOC Mission

SOC's mission statement typically includes the following elements:

1. Prevention of cybersecurity incidents through proactive:

a. Continuous threat analysis
b. Network and host scanning for vulnerabilities
c. Countermeasure deployment coordination
d. Security policy and architecture consulting

1. Monitoring, detection, and analysis of potential intrusions in real time and through historical trending on security-relevant data sources.
2. Response to confirmed incidents, by coordinating resources and directing use of timely and appropriate countermeasures.
3. Providing situational awareness and reporting on cybersecurity status, incidents, and trends in adversary behavior to appropriate organizations.
4. Engineering and operating CND technologies such as IDSes and data collection/analysis systems.

SOC Roles and Responsibilities

Security Operations Center (SOC) consists of a team of cybersecurity professionals responsible for monitoring and analyzing the potential cyber threats and respond accordingly. There are many roles in a Security Operations Center depending on the objectives an organization wants to accomplish. SOCs can range from small, five-person operations to large, national coordination centers. Some major SOC team roles are discussed in the table below:

Table 1 SOC Roles and Responsibilities

Team Member	Roles
SOC Manager	SOC Manager is responsible for managing the personnel and budget required for security solutions. They also coordinate with the legal department whenever needed.
Incident Responder	These professionals are the first ones to respond to any security incident. They perform the initial evaluation of security breaches and take appropriate actions.
Forensic Investigator	The specialists trained to analyze the attack by gathering and preserving the pieces of digital evidence.
Security Engineer	They maintain and recommend new monitoring tools to build security architecture and communicate with developers to ensure systems are up to date.
SOC Analyst	They detect, investigate, and respond to threats and can also implement additional security measures where required.

SOC Operations Overview

Operations of a SOC revolve around events. These events can be defined as "any observable occurrence in a system and/or network". These events define activities being performed on a system or network as well as sometimes provide indication that an incident is occurring. SOC collects these events which are nothing more than raw data. SOC processes these events for analysis to figure out if any anomaly or incident has been occurred. It is a challenge to collect all security related events for effective security monitoring.

Tier 1 SOC analyst is responsible for monitoring these events. If any incident or anomaly is found, these analysts escalate the initial investigation to Tier 2 SOC analyst. Usually, the time span Tier 1 takes to examine each event of interest is between 1 and 15 minutes. It depends on the SOC's escalation policy, concept of operations (CONOPS), number of analysts, size of constituency, and event volume. Tier 1 SOC analysts are not focused on in-depth analysis. They are encouraging not to miss any anomaly that come across in real-time.

In a small environment, there are thousands of events occurring per second. It could be impossible to monitor these events without any specialized tool. Security Information and Event Management (SIEM) is a popular tool which is used to collect these events from all endpoints and network devices. This tool not only collects the events from different devices integrated, but also aggregates, correlates the events and provides real-time alerts. Features and functions of SIEM are discussed in a later chapter. Apart from SIEM, there are other active and passive security controls including Intrusion Detection/Prevention Systems (IDPS), Web Application Firewalls (WAF), Next-Generation Firewalls (NGFW), Sandboxes, Endpoint Detection and Response (EDR) and Network Detection and Response (NDR). Security Engineers deploy and build security architecture using these tools for security operations.

Each case escalated to Tier 2 SOC analyst requires in-depth analysis to determine what is being happened. These analysts are more experienced than a Tier 1 analyst. They collect all necessary data for analysis, and conclude if any incident has occurred. These Tier 2 analysts are not focused for real-time monitoring; they are responsible for concluding if a potential incident has occurred.

To determine the nature of the incident, a Tier 2 analyst may forward it for forensic analysis. The Forensic Investigator performs advanced forensic analysis on the artifacts such as memory dump, hard drive images or full-session packet capture (PCAP), or malware reverse engineering on malware samples collected in support of an incident.

After identifying the incident, the role of Incident Responder comes into play. These incident responders are responsible for containing the incident, eradicating the root cause, and recovering the system to its running state. These incident responders are well-trained professional personnel who have knowledge about how to handle each incident. As per NIST SP 800-61 R2, Incident responders help personnel to minimize loss or theft of information and disruption of services caused by incidents. Another benefit of incident response is its ability to use information, gained during incident handling, to prepare for handling future incidents in a better manner and to provide stronger protection for systems and data. Incident response also helps in dealing with legal issues properly that may arise during incidents.

PUBLICANCY LTD

Figure 1 SOC Operations Overview

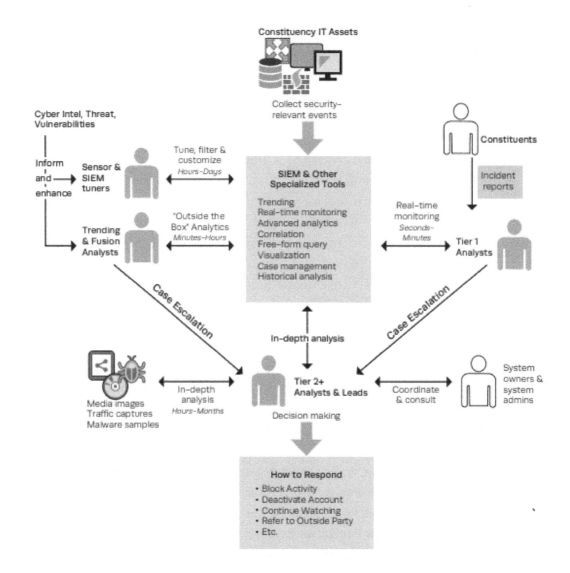

SOC Implementation Models

There are different types of SOC models. An organization can consider any of them according to its compliance requirements and budget. Different types of SOC models are discussed below:

Dedicated SOC:

Dedicated SOC is mostly approached by larger organizations or global companies. Full-time (24x7) staff of IT and cybersecurity professionals manage entire operations. This model of SOC is essential for global companies, with private data in various locations, that must comply with regulations and security policies.

Virtual SOC

Virtual SOC does not occupy a designated facility. It is based on a remote or geographically distributed team. This team becomes active when an incident occurs, running on a reactive approach. A virtual SOC is typically suited to smaller enterprises that experience only infrequent incidents and/or do not have resources for a more encompassing SOC.

Co-Managed SOC:

Co-Managed or Hybrid SOC is composed of Internal and External (Outsourced) teams. Mostly when an organization cannot operate 24x7, the hybrid SOC model can be used to reduce costs. Therefore, it is well suited for small to midsize enterprises, especially for those working extensively with third parties, and also for larger organizations and mature SOCs that can selectively outsource some security services.

Multi-Function SOC:

Multi-Function SOC includes IT/OT/ICS/NOC operations in the scope, running all critical operations from the same facility to reduce costs. This model is suitable for organizations having low risk exposure.

Components of SOC

There are three most fundamental components of SOC. These components, "People, Process, Technology" are the key to build an effective SOC. Each component has its own importance and role during security operations.

People

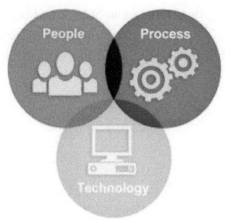

SOC needs skilled people to run their business by playing their role in the processes. These people can be organization's employees or third-party staff with defined SOC roles. An organization must define a certain criteria based on qualification, experience and skills for hiring/assigning people in SOC. These people are responsible for running the processes smoothly and efficiently. The People factor is ineffective unless the processes are defined. Following are some important people engaged in different processes:

- Security Analyst
- Security Engineer
- Threat Intelligence Analyst
- Data Scientist
- SOC Manager
- Incident Handler
- Incident Manager
- Penetration Tester
- Forensic Investigator

Process

Processes refer to business goals. The ultimate objective of all the security operations running in SOC is to keep the business running securely and uninterruptedly. These three important aspects, "people, process and technology" must be aligned with business goals. When skilled people become a part of a well-defined process, it is executed smoothly and results in a productive outcome. These processes may include:

- Shifts scheduling
- SOC management
- Incident management process
- Asset Management process
- Reporting process

Technology

Technology helps SOC not only by reducing the workload but also in achieving the hard targets. However, it is a challenge in terms of budget and Return-of-Investment (ROI). These tools help in proactively detecting threats, reducing the response time, and automating the processes. Technology component plays a vital role in an organization's cyber defense. Following are some popular technologies used in SOC:

- Intrusion Detection / Prevention System (IDPS)
- Incident Management System
- Next-Generation Firewall (NGFW)
- Security Information and Event Management (SIEM)
- Security Orchestration Automation and Response (SOAR)

Chapter 2: Cyber Threat, IoCs, and Attack Methodologies

In this chapter, you will learn about Cyber Threats, Indicators of Compromise (IoCs) and different attack methodologies.

Cyber Kill Chain

Cyber Kill Chain aka CKC is a chain of steps that traces different stages of a cyberattack from the early investigation till action on objectives. The kill chain not only helps us in hunting traditional malwares but also helps us understand and combat ransomware, data breaches, and advanced persistent threats (APTs).

There are seven core stages in the cyber kill chain:

- Reconnaissance
- Weaponization
- Delivery
- Exploitation
- Installation
- Command and Control (C2)
- Action on Objectives

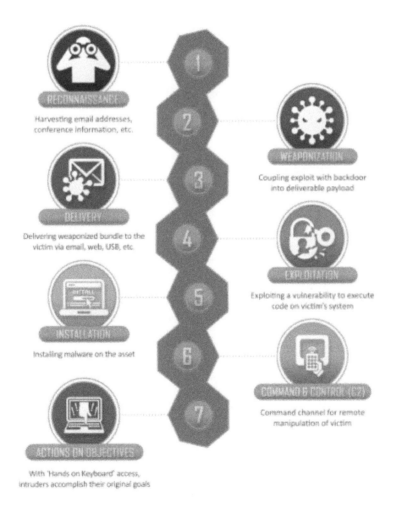

Figure 2 Cyber Kill Chain

Reconnaissance

Reconnaissance is the beginning stage where the attacker gathers information about both, the target and the tactics for the attack. Reconnaissance activities are classified into two categories:

- **Passive Reconnaissance:** Gathering information without interacting with the target such as harvesting emails, crawling the internet/public resources, dumpster diving etc.
- **Active Reconnaissance:** Gathering information by interacting with the target such as network scanning, vulnerability scanning, social engineering etc.

Weaponization

Weaponization is the next step after gathering information. Once the attacker collects sufficient information about the target and its vulnerabilities, the attacker then weaponizes against the identified vulnerability of the target. For example, after an active reconnaissance, the attacker identifies the vulnerable operating systems running in the target organization. Now, in the weaponization phase, the attacker will prepare an exploit and load it into a delivery mechanism such as a malicious executable file which can be used in evading security inspection, preparing phishing email, web hosting of malware, infecting a USB etc.

Delivery

In the delivery phase, attacker can use spear or whaling phishing technique to deliver the weaponized email to the target. Similarly, depending upon the weaponization, different techniques can be used to deliver malicious payload such as via a compromised website or a hacker-prone Wi-Fi. Intrusion is the point of entry for an attack; a way of getting the attackers inside.

Exploitation

After delivery, the next step is exploitation. There is a possibility that security control such as Email Control, WAF, NGFW blocks the malicious payload during delivery. If weaponization and delivery tactics are smart enough to evade security of the target, the malicious payload drops at the endpoint and exploits the vulnerability. Attackers often need to escalate the privileges to access resources and take full control.

Installation

In the installation phase, the malware and APTs either decompress and install themselves on the target machine or sometimes they need to download additional packages. Similarly, Remote Access Trojan creates backdoor, and changes registry keys to run on-boot in this phase to maintain persistency.

Command and Control (C2)

After installation, a communication channel is required to take over the control, exfiltrate and to conduct a denial of service. This communication is between the infected system and Command and Control. C2 communication helps the attacker to manage and modify the malicious code.

Action on Objectives

This phase depends on the malicious code, APT, and the intent of the intruder. Actions can include denial of services, data exfiltration, or transactions. In case of DOS, the objective could be reputational or financial loss. Similarly, in the case of data exfiltration, the objective could be exfiltration of confidential business contract documents, project plans or customers PII.

Cyber Threats and Attacks

A cyberattack is a deliberate malicious act by an individual or organization over the internet to breach the confidentiality, integrity or availability of information. There are different categorizations of these attacks. Keeping the architecture of an organization in consideration, cyber-attacks can be categorized as follows:

- Application Layer Attacks
- Network Layer Attacks
- Host Layer Attacks

Application Layer Attacks

Applications are one of the most critical aspect of security. There are numerous applications in an organization. Some of these applications are public-facing; intended for customers. Similarly, some applications are used internally to run operations smoothly.

From an attacker's perspective, these applications could be an entry point. These applications are either custom built or developed by a trusted party. Custom applications are needed to be quality assured against vulnerabilities. Trusted third party applications are managed and patched timely. However, an increased number of different applications raises the possibility for an attacker to find a vulnerability in the code to exploit.

Following are some application layer attacks:

Injection Attacks

Different types of injection attacks can be carried out by taking advantage of application flaws. These attacks include injection of SQL or LDAP queries to extract data from backend. Injection is basically a trick to execute unintended commands or access data by manipulating the interpreter. Through this method, the attacker can inject, extract, modify and delete critical data stored in the tables of database.

Cross-Site Scripting (XSS)

Cross-Site Scripting also takes advantage of an application's input validation flaws. If an application is not properly validating the input, the attacker can input scripts to execute. There are different types of XSS techniques such as Stored XSS in which the attacker adds malicious script in the comment section of a webpage. Similarly, an infected webpage will also execute the script whenever a user visits it. Other types of XSS include reflected, blind, and DOM-based XSS.

Application DDoS Attack

Slowloris attack is one of the popular application layer DDoS attacks. A web server receives many legitimate HTTP requests from an infected computer. The attacker keeps communicating with the web server with new partial requests on regular intervals, thus overwhelming and slowing the web server. If, in the meantime, any legitimate user wants to communicate with the web server his/her request will be refused because the web server is already overwhelmed.

Network Layer Attacks

At layer 3, there are different protocols supporting the network communication. These protocols need to be configured securely to prevent any intrusion. For example, latest versions of routing protocols support authentication but the older versions do not. Similarly, other layer 3 protocols in network communication also need to be configured in a secured way.

Man- in- the- Middle Attack

A man-in-the-middle attack is a kind of attack in which an attacker involves himself into the communication between two nodes. MITM attack can be explained as a user communicating with another user or server, and an attacker eavesdropping their communication. Replay attacks, IP and DNS Spoofing are common examples of MITM attacks.

Following are a few utilities available for attempting Man-in-the-middle (MITM) attacks:

- SSL Strip
- Burp Suite
- Browser Exploitation Framework (BeEF)

Replay Attack

In a Replay attack, an attacker mostly captures authentication packets using a packet sniffing tool. Once the authentication packets are captured, relevant information such as passwords or hashes are extracted. Later, the attacker spoofs the identity by using the captured authentication packets.

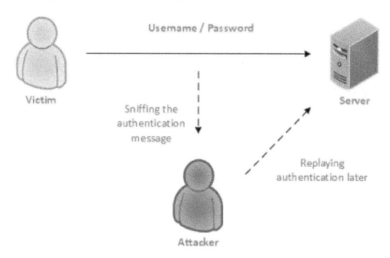

Figure 3 Replay Attack

DNS Spoofing

In DNS Spoofing, the attacker mimics a legitimate DNS server to redirect the traffic towards malicious sites. There are various methods for spoofing DNS and poisoning the cache. The Attacker may intercept requests sent from the web browser and modify them to redirect to a malicious site.

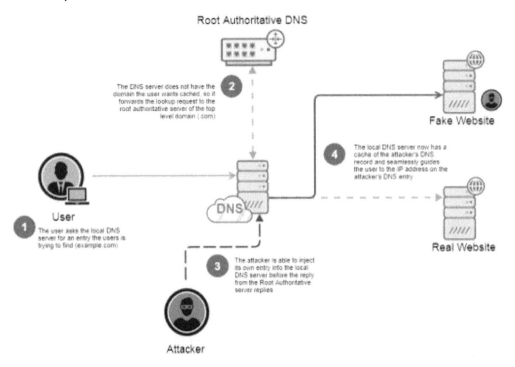

IP Spoofing

IP Spoofing is a technique in which an attacker modifies the source address of the packet. Using this method, the attacker can either hide his/her identity or impersonate any other user in the network.

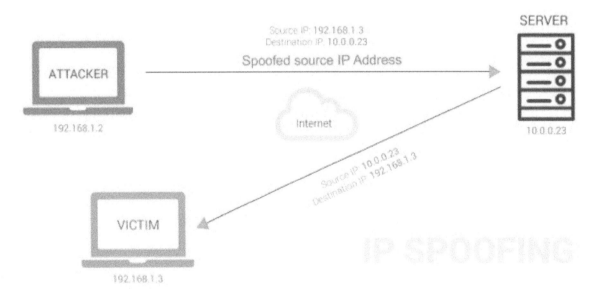

Host Level Attacks

The term malware is derived from Malicious Software. Malware is an umbrella term which defines a wide variety of potentially harmful software. This malicious software is specially designed for gaining access to target machines, stealing information, and harming the target system. Any software having malicious intention like damaging, disabling, or limiting the control of the authorized owner and providing control of the target system to the developer of malware or an attacker, or any other malicious intent can be considered as Malware.

Spyware

Spywares are the spy software designed for gathering information from a user's computer. A spy software collects email addresses, login credentials, files and other details and sends it to the attacker. Spywares are smart enough to evade detection and exfiltration.

Virus and worm

Viruses are the oldest form of malware. A virus is self-replicating; it can produce multiple copies of itself by attaching with another program of any format. These viruses can either be executed just after they are downloaded or they may be configured to execute on a triggering event (wait for the host to execute them). A virus has the following major characteristics:

- Self-Replication
- Infects other files and programs
- Transforms itself
- Encrypts itself
- May need a trigger for execution

Worm is a type of malware that is able to execute and propagate without attaching with other programs or files. Due to independency of attachment, worms propagate more rapidly than viruses.

Examples of worms:

- Sobig worm of 2003
- SQL Slammer worm of 2003
- 2001 attacks of Code Red and Nimba
- 2005 Zotob worm

Keylogger

Keylogger is also known as keystroke logger, a software program or hardware device which tracks the keystrokes and sends the typed keys to attackers. Keyloggers are a type of spyware where users are unaware of their actions being tracked.

Keyloggers can be used for a variety of purposes; hackers may use them to maliciously gain access to your private information, while employers might use them to monitor employee activities. As well as some keyloggers can capture your screen at random intervals; these are known as screen recorders. A keylogger software usually stores your keystrokes in a small file, which is either accessed later or automatically emailed to the person monitoring your actions.

Attacker's Hacking Methodology

In this section, we will discuss an attacker's hacking methodology step by step. This will help you in understanding the techniques and mindset a hacker follows to select, aim, and exploit a target.

Footprinting aka reconnaissance is the first phase of hacking in which an attacker collects information about the target. Active and passive reconnaissance is used to collect this information. Following are the different techniques used to collect information:

- OS footprinting
- Organizational Queries
- WHOIS queries
- WWW Spidering

After initial footprinting, an attacker starts scanning the target. Vulnerability scanning includes scanning vulnerable networks, ports, and devices. The attacker may discover vulnerabilities such as weak passwords, vulnerable software, firmware bugs, default configuration, etc. Similarly, other scanning tools are used to identify the configured parameters of the target network such as open ports, running protocols etc. Following is the list of some popular scanning tools:

- NMAP
- Nessus
- Nexpose
- OpenVAS
- Nikto

The attacker also collects information about network topology. It can either be performed using network topology mapping tools or observing the Time-to-Live (TTL) packets.

For enumeration, attacker builds an active connection with the target to extract usernames, devices, services, group, and other information. Normal enumeration techniques include:

- **NetBIOS Enumeration:** For extracting passwords
- **SNMP Enumeration:** For extracting network information and traffic stats
- **LDAP Enumeration:** For extracting user records

After reconnaissance and enumeration, finally the attacker moves towards the exploitation phase to gain access to the target's system using the information gathered. There different exploits which can be possible if the required information is collected by the attacker. For example, if an attacker finds an IP address of a host with an open RDP port during scanning, list of usernames and cracked the passwords during enumeration. Now, the attacker can attempt to login via RDP using the credential list. Similarly, if any vulnerable service is running over a host the attacker can exploit that service to intrude into the system.

After gaining access, obtaining privileges is the top most priority. Privileges help the attacker to perform actions easily, maintain access and persistency over the target.

At last, the attacker removes all forensic evidences to prevent back tracking. By doing this the attacker can hide his/her identity, or make it difficult for investigators to estimate the actual loss. Attackers mostly modify registry values, uninstall malicious applications and files used during exploit and delete all log entries.

Indicators of Compromise (IOCs)

Indicator of Compromise (IOC) is a piece of information which can identify the potential malicious activity on a system or network. In Information security, IOCs are served as forensic evidence of compromise. These IOCs are also used as intelligence to compare other systems if they match any indicator.

These indicators might be associated with one or more compromise activities. Hashes of malware samples, IP addresses of C2 servers, malware hosting domains, Behavior information's are used as IOCs.

Hashes, C2 IP addresses, malicious domains and URLs, phishing email addresses are updated in the firewalls, email gateways, IDPS engines to block requests from these addresses. Similarly, behaviors of malwares are contributed in the understanding of threat actors' TTPs and building detection rules.

Chapter 3: Incident, Event and Logging

In this chapter, we will discuss how to monitor and log cyber security events. Objective of monitoring security events is to correlate with potential indicators of compromise (IOC). This correlation helps finding security incidents. Each security incident has its own severity and priority as per an organization's incident priority matrix. If these incidents are not addressed on-time effectively, they can cause a huge impact on operations' continuity and business.

Events and Logging

As stated in NIST SP 800-53, an event is **any observable occurrence in an information system**. These events occurring in a system can be recorded in a log. A log is **a record of the events occurring within an organization's systems and networks**. Operating systems, applications running over an OS, databases, network devices, security devices record and maintain logging. These logs can be stored locally on the respective device as well as transported to a syslog server or SIEM.

Network and security teams monitor these security logs to identify issues, errors, potential threats, policy violations and other activities. Each endpoint system in a corporate environment generates hundreds or thousands of logs in a second; However, it depends on the auditing enabled and events being performed on that system. There are tools available to monitor this huge incoming log traffic. Event and log management tools help in ingesting logs, decoding, and indexing them in real-time. Once indexed, security teams can analyze logs by applying searches and rules and investigate security incidents.

Key concepts of log management

Logs are composed of log entries; each entry contains information related to a specific event that has occurred within a system or network. Originally, logs were used primarily for troubleshooting problems, but logs now serve many functions within most organizations, such as optimizing system and network performance, recording users' actions, and providing data useful for investigating malicious activity. Logs have evolved to contain information related to many different types of events occurring within networks and systems. Within an organization, many logs contain records related to computer security; common examples of these computer security logs are audit logs that track user authentication attempts and security device logs that record possible attacks.

Logs can contain a wide variety of information on the events occurring within systems and networks. These logs are primarily used to help detect potential cyber security incidents and/or their investigation.

In this section, following the different categories of logs of particular interest:

Types of logs	Examples
System logs	<ul><li>System activity logs (e.g. Administrator), including storage</li><li>Endpoint (and agent-based) logs</li><li>Logs from standard (e.g. SAP) and customized applications</li><li>Authentication (e.g. Windows) logs</li><li>Physical security logs</li></ul>
Networking logs	<ul><li>Email, firewall, VPN and NetFlow logs</li></ul>
Technical logs	<ul><li>HTTP proxy logs</li><li>DNS, DHCP and FTP logs</li><li>Web and SQL server logs</li><li>Appflow logs</li></ul>
Logs from cyber security monitoring and logging tools	<ul><li>Malware protection (e.g. anti-virus) logs</li><li>Network intrusion detection systems (NIDS)</li><li>Network intrusion prevention systems (NIPS)</li><li>Data loss protection (DLP)</li><li>Tools that employ potential malware isolation and investigation techniques (e.g. sandboxing or virtual execution engines)</li><li>Other relevant security management applications or tools</li></ul>

The security relevant logs should be:

- Enabled all the time.
- Logging in a standard format such as CEF, Windows Log format etc.
- Generate appropriate event types.
- Incorporate relevant event attributes in event entries (e.g. IP address, username, time and date, protocol used, port accessed, method of connection, name of device and object name).
- Use a consistent, trusted date and time source (e.g. using the Network Time Protocol; NTP, supported by global positioning).

- Protected from unauthorized access and accidental or deliberate modification or overwriting (e.g. using write-only media or dedicated event log servers).
- Configured so that when event logs reach a maximum size, the system does not halt due to lack of disk space and logging continues without any disruption.

Local Logging

Each operating system generates logs. An organization has several servers and PCs, each system will generate its own set of logs in its local directory. This is called local logging. When you configure auditing to generate and store logs, each category of log writes to a different file or database table. It might be less convenient than centralized logging because it requires you to examine multiple log locations.

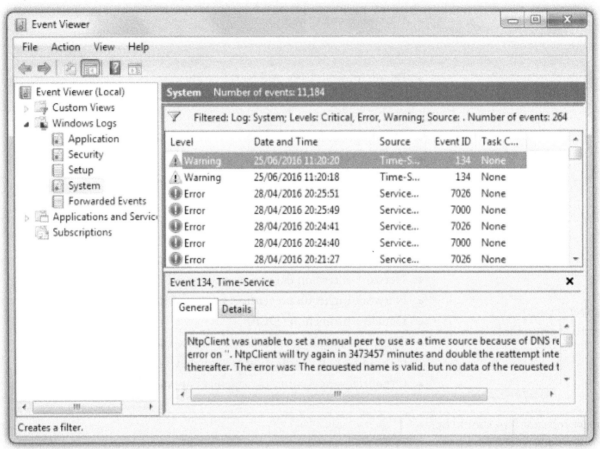

As shown in the figure above, Windows stores each category of logs in its respective directory. Following are the major categories in Windows:

- Application Logs
- Security Logs
- System Logs

Syslog

In a logging infrastructure based on the syslog protocol, each log generator uses the same high-level format for its logs and the same basic mechanism for transferring its log entries to a syslog server running on another host. Syslog provides a simple framework for log entry generation, storage, and transfer that any OS, security software, or application could use if designed to do so. Many log sources either use syslog as their native logging format that allows their log formats to be converted to syslog format.

Centralized Logging

You can configure all log sources to send logs in a central location. This concept is known as Centralized Logging. Centralized logging is the most convenient option because it allows you to view and troubleshoot all logs from a single location. Centralized logging is maintained on a log server that is specially designed to digest bulks of incoming logs continuously.

Benefits of Centralized Logging

Centralized logging is usually more suitable than local logging. Some benefits over local logging are as follows:

- Logs of all the servers are stored in a single location. To find a specific log entry, you can search a single log display. You do not need to access each server separately.
- All types of logs are stored in the same location. You do not have to search a different location for each log type.
- It is easy to manage, and backup a single central log server. This eliminates the need to backup logs from each server separately.
- Centralized logging eliminates the need to specify additional disk allocation for log retention on each server.

Chapter 4: Incident Detection with SIEM

In previous chapters, we discussed about SOC fundamentals, incidents, events, and logging. SOC collects these security events and logs into a Security Information and Event Management (SIEM) solution for analysis. SIEM is also called the heart of SOC. In this chapter, we will explore the concept of SIEM and how it is used in SOC.

Understand the Basic Concepts of Security Information and Event Management (SIEM)

Gartner defines SIEM as a technology that supports threat detection, security incident management and compliance management by analyzing security events. A SIEM solution offers a robust collection of real time security events from a wide variety of heterogeneous event sources. This collection component of SIEM forwards this queue of events to a decoder component of SIEM which normalizes these incoming events into a structured and enriched form. This structuring helps to index and perform correlation on these security events.

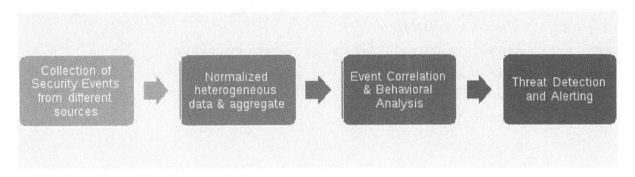

Event Sources

There are several different event sources in an environment. From SIEM's perspective, we can classify these event sources based on operating system, application, databases, network devices, security devices etc. As we know, each operating system maintains its logging in a particular directory and provides support for sending these logs to a remote server. Similarly, different default applications such as Office, PowerShell, and custom build applications such as mobile applications, web applications also support remote logging. All these event sources log security events either in their own format or in a standard logging format. Following are some examples of event sources of different categories:

Event Source Category	Event Sources
Operating System	Windows, Linux, MAC
Application	Custom applications (mobile applications, web applications)
Databases	MSSQL, MySQL
Network Devices	Routers, Gateways, Proxy
Security Devices	Firewalls, WAF, EDR

Following are log payloads of different event sources to demonstrate the need of normalization of logs. Given below, is a log payload of FortiGate firewall.

date=2017-11-15 time=11:44:16 logid="0000000013" type="traffic" subtype="forward" level="notice" vd="vdom1" eventtime=1510775056 srcip=10.1.100.155 srcname="pc1" srcport=40772 srcintf="port12" srcintfrole="undefined" dstip=35.197.51.42 dstname="fortiguard.com" dstport=443 dstintf="port11" dstintfrole="undefined" poluuid="707a0d88-c972-51e7-bbc7-4d421660557b" sessionid=8058 proto=6 action="close" policyid=1 policytype="policy" policymode="learn" service="HTTPS" dstcountry="United States" srccountry="Reserved" trandisp="snat" transip=172.16.200.2 transport=40772 appid=40568 app="HTTPS.BROWSER" appcat="Web.Client" apprisk="medium" duration=2 sentbyte=1850 rcvdbyte=39898 sentpkt=25 rcvdpkt=37 utmaction="allow" countapp=1 devtype="Linux PC" osname="Linux" mastersrcmac="a2:e9:00:ec:40:01" srcmac="a2:e9:00:ec:40:01" srcserver=0 utmref=0-220586

Similarly, below is a log payload of PaloAlto event source.

Feb 28 15:15z`:14 paloalto LEEF:1.0|Palo Alto Networks|PAN-OS Syslog Integration|4.0|HTTP Non-RFC Compliant Request(39143) |cat=THREAT| subtype=vulnerability| src=172.16.0.110| dst=13.17.13.9| srcPort=15295| dstPort=80| proto=tcp| usrName=| SerialNumber=00000000000000| srcPostNAT=172.16.18.2| dstPostNAT=13.107.136.9| RuleName=DMZ to Internet| SourceUser=| DestinationUser=| Application=web-browsing| VirtualSystem=vsys1| SourceZone=DMZ_L3| DestinationZone=Internet_L3| IngressInterface=ethernet1/8| EgressInterface=ethernet1/9| LogForwardingProfile=SIEM| SessionID=135969| RepeatCount=1| srcPostNATPort=43655| dstPostNATPort=80| Flags=0x506000| URLCategory=any| sev=informational| Severity=1| Direction=client-to-server| ContentType=| action=alert| Miscellaneous=""

Normalization

As shown above, both firewalls are logging security events in their own format. Similarly, all event sources log security events in their particular format. SIEM Solution then normalizes the logs collected from all these sources. Normalization is the process in which these incoming logs are transformed into a structured format. Relevant information from the raw payload is extracted and mapped with parsing fields. Additionally, enrichment allows to add additional contextual information to be mapped with parsing fields which helps in correlating and understanding the events.

Event Correlation & Behavioral Analysis

Event Correlation is one of the most essential components of SIEM. After aggregation and normalization of incoming events from all event sources, correlation engine of SIEM correlates these events to detect security threats and malicious behaviors. To better understand event correlation, consider a scenario where an account is used to login a few times in a day. Whenever abnormal logins are requested from the same account, behavioral analysis detects the suspicious behavior and alerts the security team. Event correlation plays an important role when a huge number of login attempts are observed followed by a successful login and access of abnormal resources which were not observed previously for that account. Event correlation helps investigating the Root Cause Analysis (RCA) by adding this context information.

Threat Detection & Alerting

SIEM also offers threat feed integration and development of custom rules to detect threats and malicious activities. With the help of correlation, behavioral analysis, intelligence feeds, and custom rules, the security team can deploy rules to automate detection of threats. Security investigators test use-cases and create rules in SIEM. These rules are applied on incoming security events to detect and alert accordingly.

SIEM Solutions & Deployment Model

Following are some popular SIEM solutions:

Splunk Enterprise Security

Splunk Enterprise Security is an analytics-driven SIEM solution that gives you the ability to quickly detect and respond to internal and external attacks. Splunk ES can be deployed as a software together with Splunk Enterprise or as a cloud service together with Splunk Cloud. Following are some key features of Splunk ES solution.

LogRhythm NextGen SIEM Platform

LogRhythm NextGen SIEM offers security analytics, network detection and response (NDR), user and entity behavior analytics (UEBA), security orchestration, and automation and response (SOAR) which makes LogRhythm a comprehensive SIEM platform. Splunk offers flexible deployment including SaaS, Cloud and On-premise options.

RSA Netwitness

NetWitness platform accelerates threat detection and response by collecting and analyzing data across more capture points (logs, packets, netflow and endpoint) and computing platforms (physical, virtual and cloud) and enriching this data with threat intelligence and business context. RSA offers extended detection and response (XDR), network & endpoint detection and response, user and entity behavior analytics (UEBA), security orchestration and automation features in Netwitness solution.

IBM QRadar

IBM QRadar also offers analytics engine to analyze network, endpoint, asset, user, vulnerability, and threat data. It includes threat intelligence from IBM X-Force, and also offers integration of additional intelligence feeds via STIX/TAXII. QRadar supports APIs and SDK to help customers ingest data faster, gain deeper insights and extend the value of existing solutions. QRadar can be delivered as hardware, software or virtual machines for on-premises or IaaS environments. Start with an all-in-one solution or scale up to a highly distributed model across multiple network segments and geographies.

AlienVault Unified Security Management

AlienVault USM is a cloud-based service which can be deployed rapidly in an environment without any need for installations and maintenance. USM uses virtual sensors for on-premises physical and virtual IT infrastructure. In the cloud, lightweight cloud sensors natively monitor cloud-based architecture. In addition, AlienVault agents help collect security events from Windows and Linux endpoints. AlienVault labs leverage data from the Open Threat Exchange® (OTX™) for continuous stream of threat intelligence.

Application Level Incident Detection Use-cases

There are different application level use-cases depending upon the environment, functions of the target application and the objective of the use-cases. Following are some most common attacks that fit in every application level incident scenario.

SQL Injection

An attacker can attempt to gain access to an application by executing malicious SQL commands on an application. These malicious SQL commands may include SQL queries to modify or delete the records in the application database. MITRE ATT&CK mapped such injection techniques as:

- T1055 Process Injection
- T1210 Exploitation of Remote Services
- T1043 Commonly used port
- T803 Block Command Message

To detect such incoming SQL queries, security teams should closely monitor application and database logs for anomalies. Application firewalls are capable of monitoring and proactively blocking these requests. The following MYSQL exploitation script shows a login bypassing trick by manipulating the SQL commands.

<username>' OR 1=1—

'OR " = ' Allows authentication without a valid username.

<username>'—

' union select 1, '<user-fieldname>', '<pass-fieldname>' 1—

'OR 1=1—

To review further scripts, please visit Github/payloadbox/sql-injection-payload-list[1]

---

1.   https://github.com/payloadbox/sql-injection-payload-list/blob/master/Intruder/exploit/MySQL/mysql-injection-login-bypass.txt

Directory Traversal

Similarly, there are other attack techniques at application layer such as Directory Traversal, also known as Path Traversal attack. In this attack, the attacker takes advantage of an application vulnerability which allows to read arbitrary files stored in the directories of an application server. These files may include application source code, credentials, keys, certificates, or other sensitive files. In some cases, write permissions are also available which allow the attacker to modify these files, so the attacker can easily take control over the application.

Following is an example of how a directory traversal attempt looks like:

http://nginx-server//////////../../

Insider Incident Detection

There are different techniques to detect suspicious behavior of insiders in an environment. To detect such incidents, different controls need to be placed in parallel. For example, if an employee leaves the organization, his/her account should be disabled immediately and SOC department should be notified that this account is not a part of the organization anymore. Whenever any resource (for example, a net share) is attempted to access by such account, security teams can respond timely.

Authentication Anomalies

Windows generates Event ID 4624 "An Account was successfully Logged on" containing Logon type 2 for interactive, 3 for network-based logon attempts. For audit failure events, Windows generates Event ID 4625 "An Account failed to log on" with failure reason in status and sub-status codes.

Microsoft-Windows-Security-Auditing,,Audit Failure,ad-01.example.com,Logon,,An account failed to log on. Subject: Security ID: S-1-0-0 Account Name: - Account Domain: - Logon ID: 0x0 Logon Type: 3 Account For Which Logon Failed: Security ID: S-1-0-0 Account Name: 901106 Account Domain: Example Failure Information: Failure Reason: Unknown user name or bad password. Status: 0xc000006d Sub Status: 0xc000006a Process Information: Caller Process ID: 0x0 Caller Process Name: - Network Information: Workstation Name: Desktop10548 Source Network Address: 172.19.28.18 Source Port: 54659 Detailed Authentication Information: Logon Process: NtLmSsp Authentication Package: NTLM Transited Services: - Package Name (NTLM only): - Key Length: 0

Table 2 Windows Logon Status Codes

Status / Sub-status Code	Failure Reason
0xC0000064	User logon with misspelled or bad user account
0xC000006A	User logon with misspelled or bad password
0xC000006F	User logon outside authorized hours
0xC0000070	User logon from unauthorized workstation
0xC0000071	User logon with expired password
0xC0000072	User logon to account disabled by administrator

For complete list of Windows Logon Status codes, please visit Microsoft Documentation for Event ID 4625(F): An account failed to log on[1]

Following threats can be monitored using the status and sub status codes given in the table above.

- Brute force attempt
- Password spray
- Suspicious attempts from a privileged account in non-business hours
- Suspicious attempts of logon from unauthorized workstation
- Logon attempts on disabled accounts

---

1.   https://docs.microsoft.com/en-us/windows/security/threat-protection/auditing/event-4625

Network Level Incident Detection

There are different techniques to inspect network traffic for anomalies. Even inspection criteria of each network device may differ depending upon the placement and connected hosts. For example, inspection criteria of incoming network traffic at Firewall placed at the perimeter of the network is different than the internal Firewall. Similarly, Firewall placed at the public DMZ will be inspected differently for threats.

Vertical Port Scanning

For example, consider a perimeter Firewall. One of the most observed threat is scanning that is observed on perimeter of the network. Security teams monitor traffic anomalies by filtering incoming traffic with respect to source IP addresses. Incoming traffic from a single IP address towards all ports is an anomaly; such behavior is known as vertical port scanning.

Horizontal Port Scanning

A single source IP attempting to connect to an entire subnet towards a unique destination port is known as horizontal port scanning. A horizontal scan is a port scan that targets the same port on several hosts. Most often the attacker is aware of a particular vulnerability and wishes to find susceptible machines. One would expect to see many horizontal scans for a particular port immediately following the publicizing of a vulnerability on that port.

Protocol Anomalies

Apart from scanning, possible exfiltration can be detected by monitoring the network traffic. A standard protocol can be abused to avoid detection of exfiltration. For example, DNS protocol is properly abused for exfiltration and C2 communication. Intruder can abuse header and payload fields to exfiltrate data mimicking normal traffic.

date=2017-11-15 time=11:44:16 type="traffic" subtype="forward" level="notice" srcip=10.1.100.155 srcname="PC1" srcport=40772 srcintf="users-interface" dstip=35.197.51.42 dstname="fortiguard.com" dstport=443 dstintf="outside-interface" proto=6 action="close" policyid=1 policytype="policy" policymode="learn" service="HTTPS" dstcountry="United States" srccountry="Reserved" trandisp="snat" transip=172.16.200.2 transport=40772 appid=40568 app="HTTPS.BROWSER" appcat="Web.Client" apprisk="medium" duration=2 sentbyte=1850 rcvdbyte=39898 sentpkt=25 rcvdpkt=37 utmaction="allow" countapp=1 devtype="Linux PC" osname="Linux"

As shown in the above sample log of a Firewall, following anomalies can be monitored:

- If Internal to External Communication towards a reported destination IP address on threat intelligence forums is found
- If a Well-known destination port is used by an unknown or known malicious application
- If a consistent connection is found with abnormal packet size

Host Level Incident Detection

Securing the host is another big challenge in this technology evolving era. As the organization grows, the number of employees, contractors and other end-users also increases connecting the organization's resources with different systems. These end hosts need to be secured from potential threats such as malware infection, exfiltration etc. This challenge becomes critical when an organization allows BYOD policy or remote working when the connecting hosts are not corporate devices.

Endpoint Detection and Response (EDR) solutions, Host based Firewalls and Anti-Virus Engines help in host level detection by installing the agent on each end host. These solutions integrate end hosts with SOC by real-time continuous monitoring and collecting the process and necessary information from the host. Monitoring the host via these solutions helps in analyzing activities and finding threats. These host level security solutions can be feed with threat intelligence and IoCs to identify threat patterns.

Following are some use-cases which can be implemented as Host level incident detection:

- Detection of usage of prohibited devices such as Tablets, Wearables etc.
- Detection of new/unregistered devices in the network.
- Detection of End-of-life / Vulnerable OS in the network.
- Detection of Malware or Indicators of threats.
- Detection of existence of malicious file / hash

Compliance Monitoring

SIEM detection rules can also be configured for compliance monitoring. For example, PCI-DSS, GDPR, HIPAA and other regulations state some criteria which organizations need to be following. SIEM can also be configured to detect compliance violation along with threat detection. Following are some high-level examples of how SIEM can help with compliance:

1- Logging visibility of critical assets
2- Monitoring changes/activities of privileged accounts
3- PII storing databases and application auditing
4- Breach notification
5- Access monitoring
6- Audit control monitoring

Chapter 5: Enhanced Incident Detection with Threat Intelligence

In this chapter, we will discuss threat intelligence, its different types and how to develop a threat intelligence strategy. We will also discuss how cyber threat intelligence and information sharing can help increase the efficiency and effectiveness of an organization's cybersecurity capabilities.

Fundamental Concepts on Threat Intelligence

Threat intelligence is the information of a threat's vectors, motives, indicators, behaviors, and properties. Threat intel may be a list of malware domains, IP addresses, websites, and other indicators of compromise (IOCs). Threat Intelligence represents a force multiplier for organizations looking to update their response and detection programs to contract with increasingly sophisticated threats. Malware is an adversary's tool, but the human is the real threat, and cyber threat intelligence emphases on countering those flexible and persistent human threats with empowered and trained human defenders.

Why threat intelligence is important?

Threat intelligence is important for the following reasons:

- It sheds light on the unknown, enabling security teams to make better decisions.
- It permits cyber security stakeholders by revealing adversarial motives and their tactics, techniques, and procedures (TTPs).
- It supports security professionals in better understanding the threat actor's decision-making process.
- It permits business stakeholders, such as executive boards, CISOs, CIOs and CTOs to invest wisely, mitigate risk, become more efficient and make faster decisions.

How a Threat Intelligence Strategy is Developed

The intelligence lifecycle is a development to transform raw data into actionable intelligence for decision making and automation. In this section, we will discuss the development and execution of an effective threat intelligence program.

Threat intelligence is inspiring because threats are continuously developing the requiring businesses to quickly adjust and take critical action. The intelligence cycle provides a background to allow cyber security teams to improve their resources and effectively respond to modern threat. There are six phases in this cycle, resulting in a feedback loop to instigate continuous improvement as shown in the figure below:

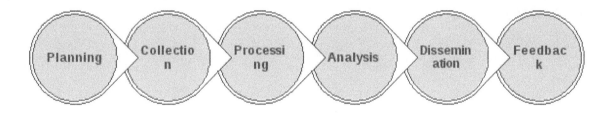

Planning

The first phase of threat intelligence lifecycle is planning. The objective to derive an actionable threat intelligence must emphasize on a single threat vector, security event or activity. The scope of intelligence must be reduced to closely estimate the impact of resulting decisions.

Prioritize your intelligence objectives based on factors like how closely they follow your organization's core values, how big of an impact the resulting decision will have, and how time sensitive the decision is.

In the planning phase, another important factor is to understand who will take advantage from the developed actionable intel — security analysts with technical skills who investigate or hunt if there is any indication of compromise in their environment? or an executive who is observing for a broad overview of trends for their upcoming security investment decisions?

Collection

The second phase is called collection phase. This phase can consume much of a TI budget by collecting raw information or data from a huge variety of sources, such as open-source threat feeds, closed threat intelligence communities, paid-for services or feeds, public forums and communities, or even human sources.

Processing

After collection, raw information is transformed into a structural form. This is known as processing. Almost all raw data collected needs to be processed in a uniform or structured manner, whether by humans or machines. Different collection approaches often require different means of processing. Collection and processing must be automated.

Analysis

In this phase, processed data is transformed into actionable information that can be further processed by the intended audience of the intelligence feeds. In a security automated environment, customers mostly need automated ingestion of threat intelligence feeds in their security controls such as SIEM, Firewalls, EDRs etc. By doing this, the need of updating the IOCs are automated.

Threat intelligence can take many forms depending on the initial objectives and the intended audience; but the idea is to get the data into a format that the audience will understand. This can range from simple threat lists to peer-reviewed reports.

Dissemination

In dissemination phase, an intelligence is created and disseminated among the customers i.e., Security Officers, Security Defenders, Security monitoring teams etc. The finalized form of intelligence will vary, depending on the subtype of intelligence and the customer.

Feedback

The final phase of the threat intelligence lifecycle includes receiving feedback on the provided report to gauge whether changes need to be made for future threat intelligence operations. Stakeholders may suggest changes according to their priorities, the time at which they demand to receive intelligence reports, or how data should be disseminated or presented.

Different Types of Threat Intelligence

Collection of information from different sources helps in identification of previously unknown threats. There is enough possibility that an unknown threat in a cycle of threat intelligence development becomes partially or fully known in the next cycle. Continuous Intelligence development helps in identification of new threats so that the internal security team can effectively mitigate the identified risks before they are exploited by the attackers.

Threat intelligence is classified into four categories:

Strategic Threat Intelligence:

Strategic Threat Intelligence is a broader term usually reserved for a non-technical audience. It is high-level information, used at board level or by other senior decision-makers. It is improbable to be technical and can cover such things as the financial impact of cyber activity, attack trends, and areas that might impact on high-level business decisions. An example would be a report demonstrating that a specific government is believed to hack into foreign companies who have direct competitors within their own nation, hence a board might consider this fact when weighing up the benefits and risks of entering that competitive marketplace, and to help them allocate effort and budget to mitigate the expected attacks. Strategic threat intelligence is almost exclusively in the form of prose, such as reports, briefings, or conversations. It is generally presented in the form of presentations, reports, conversationally or via briefings.

Operational Threat Intelligence:

In this threat, Open-Source Intelligence (OSINT) plays an important role. It is information about specific impending attacks against the organization and is initially used by higher-level security staff, such as security managers or heads of incident response. Any organization would dearly love to have true operational threat intelligence, i.e., to identify which groups are going to attack them, when and how – but such intelligence is very rare. In some cases, only a government will have the sort of access to attack groups and their infrastructure necessary to collect this kind of intelligence. For nation-state threats, it simply is not possible for a private entity to legally gain access to the relevant communication channels and hence good operational threat intelligence would not be an option for them. There are cases, however, where operational intelligence might be available, such as when an organization is targeted by more public actors, including hacktivists. It is advisable for organizations to focus on these cases, where details of attacks can be found from open-source intelligence or providers with access to closed chat forums. Another form of operational threat intelligence that might be available is the one derived from activity-based attacks; where specific activities or events in the real-world result in attacks in the cyber domain. In such instances, future attacks can sometimes be predicted following certain events. This linking of attacks to real-world events is a common practice in physical security but less commonly seen in cyber security.

Tactical Threat Intelligence:

It is also known as TTP (Tactics, Techniques, and Procedures) and is information about how threat actors are conducting attacks. Tactical threat intelligence is used by defenders and incident responders to ensure that their defenses, alert systems and investigation skills are up to the mark. For example, the fact that attackers are using tools (often Mimikatz derivatives) to obtain cleartext credentials and then replaying those credentials through PsExec is tactical intelligence that could prompt defenders to change policy and prevent interactive logins by admins, and to ensure logging will capture the use of PsExec. Tactical threat intelligence is often gained by reading white papers or the technical press, communicating with peers in other organisations to learn what they're seeing attackers do, or purchasing from a provider of such intelligence.

Technical Threat Intelligence:

It is information (or, more often, data) that is normally consumed through technical means. An example would be a feed of IP addresses suspected of being malicious or implicated as command and control servers. Technical threat intelligence often has a short lifetime as attackers can easily change IP addresses or modify MD5 sums, hence the need to consume such intelligence automatically. Technical threat intelligence typically feeds the investigative or monitoring functions of a business, by – for example – blocking attempted connections to suspected servers.

Why threat intelligence is important?

Threat intelligence is important for the following reasons:

- It sheds light on the unknown, enabling security teams to make better decisions.
- It allows cyber security stakeholders by revealing adversarial motives and their tactics, techniques, and procedures (TTPs).
- It supports security professionals to better understand the threat actor's decision-making process.
- It allows business stakeholders, such as executive boards, CISOs, CIOs and CTOs; to invest wisely, mitigate risk, become more efficient and make faster decisions.

Different Threat Intelligence Sources

An organization can improve its information security capabilities by selecting appropriate sources of intelligence. These sources can be divided into two classes i.e., internal and external sources.

Internal Sources

In an organization, there are different sources of intelligence. Different security controls having anti-virus, sandbox and correlation engines are continuously analyzing incoming traffic and alerts on any notable findings. Secondly, there are different security monitoring teams, forensic investigators and malware researchers in an organization who experience exploit kits, malware infections and other daily issues that can seem random and unconnected. They have an opportunity to build a profile of their environment by organizing such information into meaningful content. That process also gives the information security team an opportunity to learn how to turn unrelated or simple events into "enterprise intelligence." Oftentimes, gathering internal information is much easier than organizing and interpreting it.

Many organizations strive to send bulks of data to a central aggregation point, such as a SIEM system. The central aggregation point must be tuned to accept various types of data, and data must be indexed and available for query by the information security team. The team must also ensure that specific data points are being collected and alerted upon. Consider, for example, a ransomware infection delivered via spear phishing that encrypts a file share, disrupting the normal course of business and potentially causing a financial loss. Despite those negatives, the organization does not consider ransomware a targeted threat, because the situation can be easily remediated. However, by applying a TI lens to the situation, the information security team may be able to identify the path the malware took to infect the original host and what checkpoints along that path failed to detect the malware. The team can also identify vulnerabilities exploited by the malware and observe the ease with which the malware could spread internally. By polling its aggregated logs, the team could identify whether the malware caused additional damage, still yet unknown. It could also use a trivial exercise to identify gaps in its data aggregation effort and put additional collectors at those data collection points. Building and maintaining a history of incidents within an organization is a critical first step towards building a successful internal TI team. By cataloging details of the incidents, such as attack paths, vulnerabilities, malware and other network indicators, an internal team can start to recognize similarities between attack groups or malware families. This internal growth can also help the organization identify weak points, critical assets, and priorities for security policy implementation.

External Sources

Quite simply, this is intelligence that an organization acquires from outside. External TI can be further broken into multiple subgroups, including the following:

Data Feeds

Many TI vendors offer data feeds that set up a delivery mechanism for specific types of data at pre-determined intervals. Data feed sources can be further separated into subgroups and delivered in the following ways:

- Emails delivered at an interval, such as hourly, daily, or weekly
- Subscriptions that provide lists of indicators, also delivered at intervals in various formats, such as JSON or CSV
- Scripts that utilize APIs to extract information from a data source, such as a database or website
- "Special releases," such as a public report from a TI provider. The value of a feed is realized only when the receiving organization implements the data provided into its tools, including firewalls, SIEM systems, endpoint agents and network based security technologies. Data feeds may also include attacker TTPs or research reports. All of it must be consumed and acted upon by the receiving organization to extract its value.

Open-source threat intelligence (OSINT) feeds are available as well. Some organizations that monitor to look for attacker activities, such as vulnerability scanning or spam emails, aggregate their data and provide it for free. Being low cost (possibly even free) and easy to ingest, OSINT feeds can provide value to organizations. Data is often made available in multiple formats, like commercial feeds.

But OSINT feeds have their pros and cons. They are largely automated and can cause an increase in false positives. Furthermore, OSINT feeds are rarely investigation-driven and frequently rely on attackers performing a specific set of activities. However, as many attackers often exploit well-known vulnerabilities, OSINT feeds may help protect against groups scanning for these.

Commonality

Attack groups often target industries or services, as well as company by company. Organizations with similar interests, such as the financial community, have created industry-specific groups that facilitate the sharing of information. These groups, including Information Sharing and Analysis Centers (ISACs), often present findings or intelligence with higher fidelity than feeds. ISACs also help facilitate bidirectional sharing of information between the public and private sectors.

Relationships with Government and Law Enforcement

Many organizations also receive some form of TI and other benefits from relationships with government and law enforcement. For example, InfraGard is a partnership between the FBI and the private sector that provides a forum for private industry and law enforcement to confidentially share information about threats. Law enforcement agencies have also been known to provide TI to organizations, but this knowledge often arises from evidence that a breach has occurred and can be accompanied by a request for further investigation. In some cases, the information provided by law enforcement is limited due to ongoing investigations or pending litigation.

Crowdsourced Platforms

Crowdsourced TI platforms can resemble commonality sharing but serve as hubs between multiple types of entities. One reason crowdsourced platforms have become popular is that they may provide anonymous access methods. This may be useful for organizations that want to get a particular TI but not reveal their company's name and perhaps raise suspicions that they have been breached.

As with data feeds, only a small portion of the breadth of information and intelligence in a crowdsourced platform may be applicable to the acquiring organization. For example, a crowdsourced platform may provide information on an advanced threat group that is actively targeting organizations in the energy sector and provide a description of TTPs, malware and high-fidelity signatures. For an organization in the retail industry, this industry-specific information may not prove to be useful in mitigating threats. One potential drawback with crowdsourced TI platforms is that the value of the intelligence will suffer if members are minimally involved or, the data they share is generic or misleading. If data is not curated or the platform is not well maintained, data could be misclassified. An organization relying on this approach may get unreliable information and waste time and resources looking for a non-existent threat. When examining crowdsourced TI, organizations should analyze the frequency of information posted, the number of members and the reputation of the group maintaining the platform.

Combining External and Internal Sources

Both external and internal TI sources have potential applicability, but true TI harmony exists when an organization uses both sources simultaneously.

External	Internal
• What you do not know	• What you know
• How you may be attached	• How you have been attacked
• What you should be protecting	• What you are protecting

Although internal TI sources are better able to provide information that is highly relevant to the organization, external TI sources can help alert the organization about threats it was not previously aware of. These sources can also provide additional context the organization may not have. When external TI is coupled with internal TI, the organization may be able to shorten the time from infection to detection, and from detection to remediation.

Threat Intelligence Platform (TIP)

A threat intelligence platform (TIP) centralizes the collection of threat data from numerous data sources and formats it. A Threat Intelligence Platform helps organizations aggregate, act on, and analyze threat data from multiple sources in real time to support defensive actions. The most important roles of TIP are as following:

Aggregation

The ability to centralize feeds and data into a single source of truth where they can be accessed in a standardized format by anyone who needs them.

Analysis

The ability to figure out what threats are relevant to you and your team.

Action

Send the right intelligence to your detection and defense devices.

A Threat Intelligence Platform can be a cloud or on-premise system to facilitate management of threat data from a range of existing security tools such as a SIEM, Firewall, API, Endpoint management software or Intrusion Prevention System. The primary purpose is to help organizations understand the risks and protect against a variety of threat types most likely to affect their environments.

Main Features of Threat Intelligence Platform (TIP)

- Data feeds from a variety of different sources including industry groups
- Data triage
- Alerts and reports about specific types of threats and threat actors
- Analysis and sharing of threat intelligence
- Normalization and scoring of risk data

Threat Intelligence Platforms

There are different Threat Intelligence Platforms such as:

AlienVault USM

AlienVault® Unified Security Management® (USM) sends threat detection, incident response, and compliance management in one unified platform. It is considered to combine all the important security capabilities needed for effective security monitoring across cloud and on-premises environments.

CrowdStrike Falcon

CrowdStrike provides the Falcon Endpoint Protection suite, an antivirus and endpoint protection system emphasizing threat detection, machine learning malware detection, and signature free updating.

Sophos UTM

Sophos UTM delivers core Firewall features, plus sandboxing and AI threat detection for advanced network security. It has customizable deployment options.

WhoisXML API, Enterprise API and Data Feed Packages

They offer comprehensive, historical, and real-time domain, IP, and cyber intelligence.

Mimecast Threat Intelligence

Mimecast provides threat intelligence services, including the company's Threat Intelligence Dashboard, threat remediation, and the Mimecast Threat Feed for integration threat intelligence into compatible SIEM or SOAR platforms.

SolarWinds Threat Monitor

SolarWinds Threat Monitor empowers MSSPs of all sizes by reducing the complexity and cost of threat detection, response, and reporting. You become an all-in-one security operations center (SOC) that is unified, scalable, and affordable.

Cisco SecureX (formerly Threat Response)

Cisco Threat Response automates integrations across Cisco Security products and accelerates key security operation functions: detection, investigation, and remediation.

Recorded Future

Boston-based Recorded Future presents a vulnerability management solution.

Anomali ThreatStream

ThreatStream from Anomali in Redwood City speeds detection of threats by uniting security solutions under one platform and providing tools to operationalize threat intelligence.

LookingGlass Cyber Solutions

LookingGlass Cyber Solutions is a threat protection solution protecting against cyber-attacks against global enterprises and government agencies. The product is augmented by a team of security analysts who enrich the data feeds and provide timely insights to customers of potential risks.

ThreatConnect

ThreatConnect, from the company of the same name in Arlington, is described by the vendor as an Intelligence-Driven Security Operations Platform with both Security Orchestration Automation and Response (SOAR) and Threat Intelligence Platform (TIP) capabilities.

Proofpoint Domain Discover for Email

Proofpoint Domain Discover for Email provides a library and actionable intelligence of spoof and lookalike domains used to support phishing attempts against enterprise email users.

CenturyLink Analytics and Threat Management

With CenturyLink® Analytics and Threat Management services, you get the visibility needed to proactively identify potential security issues and respond to them before they cause harm.

Symantec DeepSight

Symantec DeepSight Intelligence provides timely, actionable threat intelligence enabling teams to assess risk and implement proactive controls.

Snare

Snare is an IT security analytics suite of applications from Prophecy International headquartered in Adelaide, providing a complete log monitoring and management solution, as well as network threat intelligence.

Proofpoint Nexus

Proofpoint Nexus is the security company's threat intelligence platform, now available to customers, which provides real-time data that spans email, social media, mobile devices, and SaaS applications, supporting correlative study of attack behaviors and pre-emptive or forensic exploration and analysis.

Imperva Attack Analytics

Imperva Attack Analytics, (formerly ThreatRadar), is a threat intelligence service relying on research from Imperva's Application Defense Center (ADC), integratable into Imperva's WAF solutions and able to be fed into enterprise security data.

Rapid 360

Marlabs headquartered in Piscataway offers Rapid 360, a threat intelligence platform.

Check Point ThreatCloud

Check Point Software Technologies provides threat intelligence via the Check Point ThreatCloud.

VirusTotal

Chronicle, a security company supported by Alphabet (Google), offers VirusTotal, a malware scanning and threat intelligence service.

IntSights Cyber Intelligence

IntSights is an all-in-one external threat intelligence and protection platform, purpose-built to neutralize threats outside the wire. According to the vendor, it is the only solution of its kind.

Cofense Intelligence

Cofense Intelligence delivers phishing-specific threats to help the user defend the business network. Cofense Intelligence uses proprietary techniques to analyze millions of messages daily from a wide variety of sources.

ThreatMark

ThreatMark provides fraud prevention solutions. The vendor states, major banks use ThreatMark's AI-powered technology to build secured banking experiences by validating their legitimate users across all digital channels, all while keeping the fraudsters away.

McAfee Threat Intelligence Exchange

McAfee Threat Intelligence Exchange acts as a reputation broker to enable adaptive threat detection and response. It combines local intelligence from security solutions across your organization, with external, global threat data.

McAfee MVISION Insights

MVISION Insights is designed to help organizations move to an action-oriented, proactive security posture with local and global telemetry to detect, rank, and respond quickly and accurately to threats.

Verint Web Intelligence

Verint Web Intelligence, from Verint CIS, provides for the collection and analysis of open-source data from the web, social media sites, blogs and news sites, and related sources, to support counter-terrorism and fight cyber-crime.

Menlo Security Isolation Security Operation Center(iSOC)

Menlo Security's Isolation Security Operations Center (iSOC) is a continuous threat monitoring service that complements the Menlo Security Cloud Secure Web Gateway by monitoring internet traffic that passes through the Menlo Global Cloud to identify unintended policy gaps, and misconfigurations.

Mandiant Advantage:Threat Intelligence(FireEye iSIGHT)

Threat Intelligence (replacing the former FireEye iSIGHT Threat Intelligence) is a proactive, comprehensive threat intelligence platform delivered as a subscription service, providing visibility to global threats before, during and after an attack.

Proofpoint ET Intelligence

Proofpoint Emerging Threat (ET) Intelligence provides actionable threat intel feeds to identify IPs and domains involved in suspicious and malicious activities.

Sentinel IPS

Sentinel IPS promises advanced threat protection at the network's edge with Network Cloaking™, blocking malware, exploitation attempts, and other threats before they reach the Firewall.

EclecticIQ Platform

EclecticIQ Platform is an analyst-centric Threat Intelligence Platform (TIP). The vendor says it is optimized for the collection of intelligence data from open sources, commercial suppliers, and industry partnerships into a single collaborative analyst workbench.

Webroot BrightCloud

Webroot offers the BrightCloud platform, providing a suite of threat intelligence services such as the Webroot BrightCloud Web Classification and Reputation Services, Webroot BrightCloud IP Reputation Service, the Webroot BrightCloud Real-Time Anti-Phishing Service.

Kaspersky Private Security Network

Kaspersky Labs offer threat intelligence as a service, but for those who prefer a secure on-premise technology-based solution, the company also provides Kaspersky Private Security Network; a threat intelligence platform supporting network security apps, appliances, and other Kaspersky security software.

Palo Alto Networks AutoFocus

AutoFocus™ contextual threat intelligence service, from Palo Alto Networks, accelerates analysis, correlation, and prevention workflows. Targeted attacks are automatically prioritized with full context, allowing security teams to respond to critical attacks faster, without additional IT security resources.

IBM X-Force

IBM experts provide the X-Force threat intelligence suite of services, including X-Force Research and X-Force Research Publications, and the X-Force Exchange platform for sharing threat intelligence knowledge and best practices with industry experts.

IBM X-Force Incident Response and Intelligence Service(IRIS)

IBM X-Force IRIS can be deployed on-site to provide a complete cybersecurity incident response, threat intelligence, and breach remediation platform.

Exabeam Security Management Platform

Exabeam headquartered in San Mateo, offers their SIEM platform; The Exabeam Security Management Platform. The vendor states, the modular Exabeam platform allows analysts to collect unlimited log data, use behavioral analytics to detect attacks, and automate incident response.

Chapter 6: Incident Response

In this chapter, we will discuss how an active incident response process takes place. In Cyber Security, incident response lifecycle is one of the most critical and continuous process. Different people with different expertise are engaged, working together to be prepared to handle an incident until it is properly responded to. The main emphasis of this chapter is on detecting, analyzing, prioritizing, and handling incidents.

Fundamental Concepts of Incident Response

Incident response is a defined strategy of an organization which is used to identify and deal with cybersecurity incidents. NIST SP 800-61R2 defines 4 steps of incident response lifecycle which are discussed later in this chapter. A computer security incident is an imminent threat of violation of computer security policies, acceptable use policies, or standard security practices.

Examples of incidents are:

- An attacker commands a botnet to send high volumes of connection requests to a web server, causing it to crash.
- Users are tricked into opening a "quarterly report" sent via email that, in reality, is malware; running it infects their computers and establishes connections with an external host.
- An attacker obtains sensitive data and threatens that the details will be released publicly if the organization does not pay a designated sum of money.
- A user provides or exposes sensitive information to others through peer-to-peer file sharing services.

Attacks often compromise personal and business data, and it is critical to respond rapidly and effectively when security breaches occur. The concept of computer security incident response has become widely accepted and implemented. Benefit of an incident response is that it supports responding to incidents thoroughly (i.e., following a consistent incident handling methodology) so that the appropriate actions are taken. Incident response helps personnel to minimize loss or theft of information and disruption of services caused by incidents. Another benefit of incident response is the ability to use information gained during incident handling to better prepare for handling future incidents and to provide stronger protection for systems and data. It also helps in dealing properly with legal issues that may arise during incidents.

Various Phases in Incident Response Process

NIST SP 800-61 R2 is about handling computer security incidents and it has defined the entire lifecycle of incident response. NIST IR lifecycle consists of 4 sequential phases which are aligned from preparation till post-incident activities. Following figure highlights the phases of NIST IR lifecycle.

Preparation

The preparation phase is about taking necessary measures. Organizations prepare security strategies, policies, and plans, define security roles and escalation matrix to be prepared operationally. This phase also deals with technical preparation such as placing appropriate security controls which can help in detecting, preventing, blocking, and providing visibility for security teams.

Following are some key preparation steps that an organization should cover:

- Defining Incident Response Policy, Escalation matrix and Point of Contacts list
- Segregating and assigning duties of IR team
- Preparation of Investigation and Forensic workstations for IR teams
- Preparing inventory of critical assets, list of privileged accounts etc.
- Endpoint, Network and Perimeter hardening
- Training of IR teams

Incident response policy is specific to an organization. It depends on the nature of business, type of threats to a particular organization. Following are some aspects that should be covered in an incident response policy:

- Purpose and Objectives
- Scope of the policy (to whom and to what it applies and under what circumstances)
- Definition of incidents and related terms
- Organizational structure and definition of roles, responsibilities, and levels of authority
- Requirements and guidelines for external communications and information sharing (e.g., what can be shared with whom, when, and over what channels)
- Handoff and escalation points in the incident management process
- Prioritization or severity ratings of incidents
- Reporting and contact forms

Organizations should also have a formal, focused, and coordinated approach for responding to incidents, such as incident response workflow that provides the roadmap for implementing the steps of incident response. Every organization needs such a defined flow which fits in the organization's structure, and functions. An incident response workflow should include the following elements:

- Organizational step-by-step approach to handle an incident
- Metrics for measuring the incident response capability and its effectiveness
- Escalation criteria and communication guidelines

Detection & Analysis

Incident detection and analysis would be easy if every indicator were sure to be accurate; unfortunately, this is not the case. For example, user-provided indicators such as a complaint of a server being unavailable are often incorrect. Intrusion detection systems may produce false positives — incorrect indicators. These examples validate what makes incident detection and analysis so tough; each indicator should be evaluated to check if it is legitimate. Making matters worse, the total number of indicators may be thousands or millions a day. Finding the real security incidents that happened out of all the indicators can be a daunting task.

Some incidents are easy to detect by the system, such as an obviously defaced web page. However, many incidents are not connected with clear symptoms. Small signs such as one change in one system configuration file may be the only indicator that an incident has happened. In incident handling, detection may be the most tough task. Incident handlers are responsible for analyzing ambiguous, contradictory, and incomplete symptoms to check what has happened. While technical solutions exist that can make detection easier, the best preparation is to build a team of highly experienced and proficient staff members who can analyze the precursors and indicators effectively and efficiently and take proper actions. Without a well-trained and capable staff, incident detection and analysis will be conducted inefficiently, and costly mistakes will be made.

The incident response team must work rapidly to analyze and validate each incident, following a predefined process and documenting each stage. When the team believes that an incident has happened, it must quickly perform an initial analysis to control the incident's scope, such as which networks, systems, or applications are important; who or what invented the incident; and how the incident is occurring (e.g., what tools or attack methods are being used, what vulnerabilities are being exploited). The initial analysis should offer enough information for the team to arrange subsequent events, such as containment of the incident and deeper analysis of the properties of the incident. Executing the initial analysis and validating it is challenging. There are some recommendations for making incident analysis easier and more effective such as:

Profile Networks and Systems. Profiling is measuring the features of expected activity so that changes to it can be more easily identified. Examples of profiling are running file integrity, checking software on hosts to derive checksums for critical files and monitoring network bandwidth usage to determine what the average and peak usage levels are on various days and times. In preparation, it is hard to detect incidents accurately using most profiling techniques; organizations should use profiling as one of several detection and analysis techniques.

Understand Normal Behaviors. Incident response team members must study networks, systems, and applications to recognize what their normal behavior is so that abnormal behavior can be documented more easily. No incident handler will have a complete knowledge of all behavior throughout the environment, but handlers would know which experts could fill in the gaps. One system to gain this knowledge is through reviewing log entries and security alerts. This may be dull if filtering is not used to condense the logs to a reasonable size. As handlers become more familiar with the logs and alerts, they must be able to concentrate on unexplained entries, which are regularly more important to investigate. Conducting frequent log reviews must keep the knowledge fresh, and the analyst must be able to notice trends and changes over time. Reviews also give the analyst an indication of the reliability of each source.

Create a Log Retention Policy. Information regarding an incident may be recorded in several places, such as Firewall, IDPS, and application logs. Creating and implementing a log retention policy that specifies how long log data should be maintained may be tremendously helpful in analysis because older log entries may show reconnaissance activity or previous instances of similar attacks. Another purpose for retaining logs is that incidents may not be discovered until days, weeks, or even months later. The length of time to maintain log data is dependent on numerous factors, including the organization's data retention policies and the volume of data.

Perform Event Correlation. Evidence of an incident may be captured in several logs. Each log contains different kinds of data — a Firewall log may have the source IP address that was used, whereas an application log may contain a username. A network IDPS may detect that an attack was launched against a particular host, but it may not know if the attack was successful. The analyst may need to examine the host's logs to control that information. Correlating events among various indicator sources can be invaluable in validating whether a particular incident happened.

Keep All Host Clocks Synchronized. Protocols such as the Network Time Protocol (NTP) synchronize clocks among hosts. Event connection will be more complex if the devices reporting events have unpredictable clock settings. From an evidentiary standpoint, it is better to have consistent timestamps in logs—for example, to have three logs that show an attack happened at 12:07:01 a.m., rather than logs that list the attack as happening at 12:07:01, 12:10:35, and 11:07:06.

Maintain and Use a Knowledge Base of Information. The knowledge base should include information that handlers need for referencing quickly during incident analysis. Although it is possible to build a knowledge base with a complex structure, a simple approach can be effective. Text documents, spreadsheets, and simple databases run active, flexible, and searchable mechanisms for sharing data among team members. The knowledge base must also cover a variety of information, including explanations of the significance and validity of precursors and indicators, such as IDPS alerts, operating system log entries, and application error codes.

Use Internet Search Engines for Research. Internet search engines can help analysts find information on unusual activity. For example, an analyst may see some unusual connection attempts targeting TCP port 22912. Performing a search on the terms "TCP," "port," and "22912" may return some hits that contain logs of similar activity or even an explanation of the significance of the port number. Note that separate workstations must be used for research to minimize the risk to the organization from conducting these searches.

Run Packet Sniffers to Collect Additional Data. Sometimes the indicators do not record enough detail to permit the handler to understand what is occurring. If an incident is happening over a network, the fastest system to collect the necessary data may be to have a packet sniffer capture network traffic. Configuring the sniffer to record traffic that matches detailed criteria must keep the volume of data controllable and minimize the inadvertent capture of other information. Because of privacy concerns, some organizations may require incident handlers to request and receive permission before using packet sniffers.

Filter the Data. There is simply not sufficient time to review and analyze all the indicators; at minimum the most suspicious activity must be investigated. Real strategy is to filter out types of indicators that tend to be insignificant. Another strategy is to show only the types of indicators that are of the highest significance; however, this approach carries substantial risk because new malicious activity may not fall into one of the chosen indicator types.

Seek Assistance from Others. Occasionally, the team will be unable to control the full cause and nature of an incident. If the team lacks enough information to contain and eradicate the incident, then it should consult with internal resources (e.g., information security staff) and external resources (e.g., US-CERT, other CSIRTs, contractors with incident response expertise). It is significant to accurately control the cause of each incident so that it can be fully contained and the exploited vulnerabilities can be mitigated to prevent similar incidents from happening.

Containment, Eradication, and Recovery

Containment is significant before an incident overwhelms resources or increases damage. Most incidents require containment, so it is important to contain it as early as possible. Containment offers time for developing a tailored remediation strategy. An important part of containment is executive (e.g., Isolating a system from a network, disabling certain functions). Such results are much easier to obtain if there are fixed strategies and procedures for containing the incident. Organizations must explain acceptable risks in dealing with incidents and develop strategies consequently. Containment strategies vary based on the category of incident. For example, the strategy for containing an email-borne malware infection is quite different from that of a network-based DDoS attack. Organizations must create separate containment strategies for each major incident category, with criteria documented visibly to facilitate executive. Criteria for defining the appropriate strategy includes:

- Potential damage and theft of resources
- Need for evidence preservation
- Service availability (e.g., network connectivity, services provided to external parties)
- Time and resources needed to implement the strategy
- Effectiveness of the strategy (e.g., partial containment, full containment)
- Duration of the solution (e.g., emergency workaround to be removed in four hours, temporary workaround to be removed in two weeks, permanent solution).

In some cases, organizations transmit the attacker to a sandbox (a form of containment) so that they can monitor the attacker's activity, generally to gather additional evidence. The incident response team must discuss this strategy with its legal department to check if it is feasible. Behaviors of monitoring an attacker's activity other than sandboxing should not be used; if an organization knows that a system has been compromised and enables the compromise to continue, it may be responsible if the attacker uses the compromised system to attack other systems. The delayed containment strategy is risky because an attacker could escalate unauthorized access or compromise other systems.

After an incident has been contained, **eradication** may be required to eliminate components of the incident, such as cleaning the malware infection and disabling breached user accounts, also identifying, and mitigating all vulnerabilities that were exploited. During eradication, it is significant to categorize all affected hosts within the organization so that they can be remediated. For some incidents, eradication is either not required or is executed during recovery.

In **recovery**, administrators return systems to normal operation, authorize that the systems are functioning usually, and (if valid) remediate vulnerabilities to prevent similar incidents. Recovery may include activities such as restoring systems from clean backups, rebuilding systems from scratch, replacing compromised files with clean versions, installing patches, changing passwords, and tightening network perimeter security (e.g., Firewall rulesets, boundary router access control lists). Higher levels of system logging or network monitoring are often part of the recovery process. When a resource is attacked once, it is often attacked again, or other resources within the organization are attacked in a similar manner.

For large-scale incidents, recovery may take months; the intent of the early phases must be to increase the overall security with comparatively rapid (days to weeks) high value changes to prevent future incidents. The later phases must emphasize on longer-term changes (e.g., infrastructural changes) and ongoing work to make the enterprise as secure as possible.

Post-Incident Activity

Post-Incident Activity is one of the most significant parts of incident response is also the most often except: learning and improving. Each incident response team must change to reflect new threats, improved technology, and lessons learned. Holding a "lessons learned" meeting with all complicated parties after a main incident, and optionally sometimes after lesser incidents, can be helpful in improving security measures and the incident handling process itself. Various incidents can be covered in a single, lessons learned meeting. This meeting offers a chance to achieve closure with respect to an incident by reviewing what occurred, what was done to intervene, and how well intervention worked.

How to Respond to an Incident

There are many kinds of incidents in computer networks. For some organizations, a violation of a policy can also be considered and treated as an incident. Among cyber security incidents, the classification could be ranging from an internal threat to a state-sponsored cyber-attack.

In this section, we will discuss cyber security incidents and how to respond to them in an organization. The main difference between different kinds of cyber security incidents appears to lie in the source of the incident (e.g. a minor criminal compared to a major organized crime syndicate), rather than the kind of incident (e.g. hacking, malware or social engineering). Thus, it may be useful to explain cyber security incidents based on the kind of attacker, their capability and intent.

The "Cyber Kill Chain" is a categorization of phases required for an attacker to successfully infiltrate a network and exfiltrate data from it. Each phase determines a specific goal along the attacker's path. Designing your monitoring and response plan around the cyber kill chain model is an effective process because it emphasizes on how actual attacks occur.

Phases	Attacker's Goal
Reconnaissance & Probing	• Find target • Develop plan of attack based on opportunities for exploit
Delivery Attack	• Place delivery mechanism online • Use social engineering to induce target to access malware or another exploit
Exploitation & Installation	• Exploit vulnerabilities on target systems to acquire access • Elevate user privileges and install persistence payload
System Compromise	• Ex-filtrate high-value data as quietly and quickly as possible • Use compromised system to gain additional access, "steal" computing resources, and/or use in an attack against someone else

There are different types of network security incidents such as:

Incident Type	Kill Chain Stage	Recommended Action
Port Scanning Activity	Reconnaissance & Probing	Ignore most of these events UNLESS the source IP has a known bad reputation, and there are multiple events from this same IP in a small timeframe.
Malware Infection	Delivery & Attack	Remediate any malware infections as quickly as possible before they progress. Scan the rest of your network for indicators of compromise associated with this outbreak (e.g., MD5 hashes).
Distributed Denial of Service	Exploitation & Installation	Configure web servers to protect against HTTP and SYN flood requests. Coordinate with your ISP during an attack to block the source IPs.
Distributed Denial of Service Diversion	Exploitation & Installation	Sometimes a DDoS is used to divert attention away from another more serious attack attempt. Increase monitoring & investigate all related activity, and work closely with your ISP or service provider.
Unauthorized Access	Exploitation & Installation	Detect, monitor, and investigate unauthorized access attempts – with priority on those that are mission-critical and/or contain sensitive data.
Insider Breach	System Compromise	Identify the privileged user accounts for all domains, servers, apps, and critical devices. Ensure that monitoring is enabled for all systems, and for all system events, and make sure it is feeding your log monitoring infrastructure (your USM or SIEM tools).
Unauthorized Privilege Escalation	All Stages	Configure your critical systems to record all privileged escalation events and set alarms for unauthorized privilege escalation attempts.
Destructive Attack	System Compromise	Backup all critical data and systems. Test, document, and update system recovery procedures. During a system compromise - capture evidence carefully, and document all recovery steps as well as all evidentiary data collected.
Advanced Persistent Threat	All stages	Any one of the singular events that are listed here could be a part of the worst type of security incident imaginable... the dreaded APT. The important thing is to view each event through a larger context, one that incorporates the latest threat intelligence

Following are steps of a response plan for an incident:

1. Classifying a suspected cyber security incident (e.g., monitoring evidence of rare occurrences and assessing one or more trigger points)
2. Creating the aims of any investigation and clean-up operation
3. Examining all available information connected to the potential cyber security incident
4. Defining what has occurred (e.g., a DDOS, malware attack, system hack, session hijack, data corruption etc.)
5. Classifying what systems, networks, and information (assets) have been compromised
6. Defining what information has been disclosed to unauthorized parties, stolen, deleted or corrupted
7. Finding out who did it (i.e., which threat agent or agents); and why (e.g., financial gain, hacktivism, espionage, revenge, challenge or just for fun)
8. Working out how it occurred (e.g., how did the attacker gain entry to the system)
9. Defining the potential business effect of the cyber security incident
10. Accompanying sufficient investigation (e.g., using deep dive forensic capabilities) to recognize (and prosecute, if appropriate) the perpetrator(s).

Moreover, few organizations are well organized for a cyber security incident in terms of:

- People (e.g., an incident response team or individual, technical experts, fast access to decision-makers, representation from key suppliers)
- Process (such as knowing what to do, how to do it and when to do it – e.g., when detecting, containing, eradicating, or recovering from a cyber security incident)
- Technology (e.g., knowing their network topology, providing the right event logs)
- Information (e.g., having information close to hand about business operations and priorities; critical assets; and key dependencies, such as on third parties, important locations or where relevant information resides).

To build an effective cyber security incident response capability, it can be useful to examine what you may need to do before, during and after a cyber security attack. There are three phases of cyber security incident. They are demonstrated in the figure below:

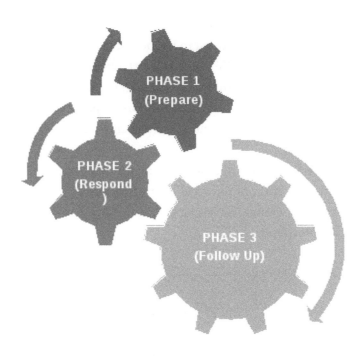

Phase 1: PREPARE

After dealing with a cyber security incident, the most significant actions are to be accurately prepared. This will help you to improve your systems more rapidly, minimize the influence of the attack, introduce confidence in your customers and even save you money in the long period. This first stage is critical, but can easily be ignored because of lack of awareness, support or resources.

To be well prepared, you must be able to control the criticality of your key resources; analyze threats to them; and implement a set of complimentary controls to provide an appropriate level of protection. As the implications of people, process, technology, and information; you can then inform your cyber security response capability and review your state of readiness in cyber security response.

Stage 1: Conduct a critical assessment

Organizations faced the five challenges of research when making the essential risk assessment and awareness arrangements to support them prepare for a cyber security incident are following as:

1. Identify and list their critical information assets
2. Identifying threats to each critical asset
3. Application of security measures to reduce the exposure of each critical asset
4. Raising security awareness among technical and non-technical staff
5. Defining the likelihood and impact associated with the possible threats
6. Proper classification of critical assets and defining the asset owners

Research exposed that many organizations often did not know the criticality of their own resources and failed to carry out business impact analysis making it hard to control how to protect these resources before, during and after a cyber security incident. You must, therefore, carry out a risk assessment to classify your critical data resources (e.g., important business applications, key systems, and confidential data), for example in terms of their strategic value. The potential harm that can be caused if your organization was hit by a cyber security incident must then be determined. This is classically realized by carrying out a business impact assessment – concentrating on confidentiality, integrity, and availability – defining the level of business impact if:

- Sensitive information was revealed to unauthorized parties (confidentiality)
- Important information was compromised (e.g., key data is inaccurate or wrongly managed)
- Dangerous systems or infrastructure were no longer accessible.

When defining business effects, it is convenient to consider scenarios and classify any serious implications in the event of a cyber security incident compromising your critical assets, such as:

- Potential and actual financial loss
- Compliance implications (e.g., fines, business restrictions, or other penalties)
- Damage to reputation
- Loss of management control
- Impaired growth

When you have identified your critical resources, you must control where they are located in your organization (and beyond), and record important details about their level of criticality (e.g., critical, significant, minor or negligible). Finally, you must assign responsibility for protecting these assets to capable, named individuals.

Stage 2: Carry out Threat Analysis

Now the next stage in being prepared for a cyber security incident is to know the level of threat to your organization, which is often completed by carrying out a threat analysis. To do this, you must produce an explanation of what an incident means to your organization and create a set of cases of the varieties of threats associated with these incidents, such as exploitation, malware infection, and exfiltration.

To contextualize the cyber security threat analysis, you will need to gain a solid considerate of the:

- Nature of your business, business strategy, business processes and risk appetite
- Key needs of your organization; for example, people, technology, suppliers, partners, and the environment in which you activate.
- Resources that are possible to be targeted, such as infrastructure, money, intellectual property, or people – and the computer systems that support them
- Potential compromise to the confidentiality of sensitive data; the integrity of important business data and applications; or the availability of critical infrastructure.

Behavior in mind these important business elements, you can then emphasis the threat analysis on the:

- Technical infrastructure that supports your critical resources
- Cyber security landscape applicable to your organization
- Different kinds of cyber security threats that you are concerned about
- Sources of these threats, such as organized crime syndicates, state-sponsored organizations, extremist groups, hacktivists.
- Conceivable threat vectors for attacks to exploit (e.g., Internet downloads, unauthorized USB sticks, misconfigured systems, inappropriate access, or collusion)
- Vulnerabilities to each specific threat (e.g., control weaknesses or special circumstances).

Stage 3: Implications of People, Process, Technology, and Information

Organizations face another challenge when making the essential arrangements to help them prepare for an incident. These essential arrangements include People, Process, Technology, and Information because they are significant to address during the preparation phase.

People

Organizations often do not have a formal incident response team or even a named individual who is responsible for dealing with such an incident. More important can be that there is often a lack of technical expertise and nobody available to make business decisions quickly.

Process

Many organizations do not have reliable processes (if they have any at all) to support them deal with incidents in a fast, effective, and reliable manner. They struggle to know what to do, how to do it, who to contact and can even compromise investigations by their activities.

Technology

Many organizations have not arranged their systems or networks to support them recognize or respond to incidents, with inadequate monitoring processes in place. To be precise, systems may not have been arranged to record proper events, classify possible attacks, or provide adequate assistance to investigators.

Information

Organizations rarely have information readily accessible that will support the investigation of an incident by response team (including third party experts) to respond rapidly and effectively, such as details about business management; IT infrastructure; key suppliers; sensitive data; and event logging.

Stage 4: Create an appropriate control environment

There are different security controls which can be implemented at different layers to help protect the organization by decreasing the possibility of an incident occurring in the first place, such as access control, malware protection systems, firewalls, and sandbox. Even if these technical controls do not prevent cyber security attacks, they can frustrate a determined attacker – providing further period for detection before the attack becomes critical.

There are several controls that seem to be mainly helpful in reducing the possibility of some kinds of cyber security attacks, such as:

- Multi factor authentication like, something you know (e.g., a User ID and password) and something you have (e.g., an access, bank, or smart card)
- Digital certificates used to "symbol" code from a vendor so that the code can be trusted
- Whitelisting (defining all acceptable ports, addresses – and preventing all other access) or blacklisting (preventing access from specific sites, or addresses)
- Technical monitoring tools, such as intrusion detection or prevention systems (IDS and IPS), data loss preventions (DLP) systems and searchable incident event repository (SIEM).

More advanced controls – which are often only accepted by larger or more critical organizations as they are classically complex, expensive, and resource intensive including:

- Continuous monitoring
- Proactive threat hunting
- Outbound gateway consolidation
- System virtualization
- Sensitive network or data segregation
- Counterintelligence operations.

Stage 5: Review your state of readiness

It is significant that your organization maintains an appropriate incident response capability. This must consist of properly skilled people guided by well-designed processes that allow the effective use of applicable technologies. Having the right capability can help you to conduct a thorough investigation and effectively eradicate adversaries who are deeply embedded in your environment.

However, many organizations do not identify their state of readiness to be able to respond to a cyber security incident in a fast, effective manner. One of the ways to help control your state of readiness is to measure the level of maturity of your Incident Response capability in terms of:

- People, process, technology, and information
- Preparedness, response and follow up activities.

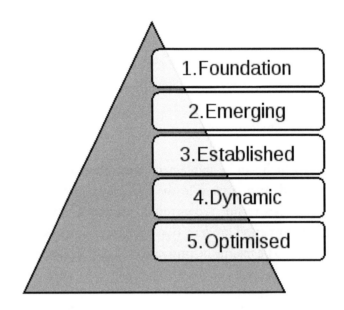

The maturity of your Incident Response can play an important role in defining the level of third-party involvement during a breach investigation and eradication event. Organizations with mature Incident Response may conduct most of their operations in-house, while those who are less mature may depend entirely on third parties.

Phase 2: Respond

There are some stages that Incident Response specialists follow to help them handle an incident well, which must be part of a wider tactic, with an importance on investigation. Therefore, to offer you with a wider considerate of a representative live situation, following stages have been developed:

Stage 1: Identify cyber security incident

For many organizations, the most interesting part of the incident response method is detecting and assessing conceivable incidents - defining whether an incident has happened and, if therefore, the category, range, and magnitude of the problem.

Organizations face four challenges when trying to classify an incident in a fast, effective, and consistent manner. Those are as following:

- Classifying a suspected cyber security incident (e.g., monitoring sign of unusual occurrences and assessing one or more trigger points)
- Evaluating all accessible information associated to the potential cyber security incident
- Defining what has actually occurred (e.g., a malware attack, DDOS, system hack, data corruption or session hijack)
- Confirming that they have been subject to a cyber security attack or had a cyber-related breach (the unknown element).

Detecting potential Incidents

Incidents may take place over a long timeframe and / or in different zones of the organization. Advanced targeted attacks can go undetected for several months or years, and even when exposed are expected to be nothing more than a common malware infection. Equally, many alternatives of credential stealing Trojans can remain undetected for various months at a time.

There are many different methods through which a cyber security incident can be recognized (with changeable levels of detail and accuracy), they are:

- Alerts produced by technical monitoring systems, such as Data Loss Prevention (DLP), intrusion detection systems (IDS), antivirus software, and log analyzers
- Doubtful events reported, for example, to the IT help desk by operators; to account managers by third parties (often customers); or directly to the security team by industry forms, your vendor partners, or the government
- Anomalies detected by audits, reviews, or investigations.

Incidents can be detected in any part of the organization or through third parties. You must, therefore, confirm that your Incident Response method is suitably broad and highlight the importance of incident detection and analysis throughout the organization.

Workers should be informed that they must:

- Report all suspected cyber security breaches to a central point (e.g., information failures; loss of services; detection of malicious code; denial of service attacks; errors from incomplete or inaccurate business data)
- Note all significant details (e.g., kind of breach, messages on screen, details of unusual occurrences)
- Restrain from trying to take remedial activities themselves

Stage 2: Define objectives and investigate situations

Once an incident has been detected, the next stage is to identify the legitimacy and scope of infection. There are numerous questions that investigators must seek to answer, such as:

- Who has attacked us?
- What is the scope and extent of the attack?
- When did the attack happen?
- What did the attackers take from us?
- Which systems / users are compromised?
- Why did they do it?
- How did they do it?

Organizations face three main challenges when responding to an Incident in a fast, effective, and consistent manner. Those are as following:

- Estimating the scope of infection
- Identifying the loss and estimating the impact of compromise
- Identifying the source of attack

Other important response challenges involve:

- Working out how it occurred (e.g., how did the attacker enter into the system)
- Defining the potential business impact of the incident
- Execution and complete analysis of the incident

When exploring the incident, you must learn as much as you can about the attacker as they will need different response methods and capabilities. You must determine what:

- Latest TTPs of attackers (attack methodologies, point of entry)
- Intentions and motivations of attackers (Money, Reputation loss, Disruption)
- Emphasis (e.g., an individual, the complete organization, your market sector, or the government).

Stage 3: Take appropriate action

Containment

After the initial investigation, one of the first key actions (as part of response) is to cover the damage caused by the incident, for example by stopping it from distributing to other networks and devices both within your organization and beyond.

Containment contains a number of concurrent actions intended at reducing the instantaneous influence of the Incident, mainly by eliminating the attacker's access to your systems. The objective of containment is not always to return to business as usual, but to make best efforts to prevent further propagation of infection, although continuing to analyze the incident and plan longer term remediation.

There are several methods in which an incident can be contained, those are as follows:

- Blocking intruder's IP address
- Temporarily disabling the compromised user accounts
- Blocking malware IoCs (e.g., Malicious URLs, Domains, Hashes)
- Isolating the system from the network
- Firewall filtering

You must consider creating separate containment strategies for different types of major cyber security attacks, with criteria documented clearly to facilitate decision-making. These criteria can include evaluating the:

- Potential damage to and theft of resources
- Need for evidence preservation
- Service availability (e.g., network connectivity, services provided to external parties)
- Time and resources needed to implement the strategy
- Effectiveness of the strategy (e.g., partial containment, full containment)
- Duration of the solution (e.g., emergency workaround to be removed in four hours, temporary workaround to be removed in two weeks, permanent solution).

Eradication

When an incident has been contained, eradication is often essential to remove infection of the incident (e.g., removing the malicious files, malwares from the infected systems, killing the running malicious processes, and resetting the modifications), and identifying and mitigating vulnerabilities that were exploited.

During the eradication process, there are a number of actions you can take:

- Running malware scan on all infected hosts / users to eradicate infection
- Malware analysis on infected host
- Killing malicious processes / scheduled tasks

There are various steps that attackers take to either avoid identification or continue the attack during eradication, which contain:

- Recording new IP addresses for their domain names if they suspect that eradication teams have blocked their IP addresses
- Accessing an undetected web shell, they have installed earlier to recover access to the environment after access has been removed
- Installing advanced malware that makes changes to the file system or network to trigger a fail-safe within the malware if detected, which will in turn remove itself together with the evidence of infection.

Gathering and preserving evidence

Research indicated that organizations have difficulty in meeting forensic necessities for incident response, such as in protective evidence and keeping a chain of custody.

In each response step, evidences will be gathered, but all evidence will be governed by two main rules, which are as following:

- Admissibility of evidence (whether the evidence can be used in court)
- Weight of evidence (the quality and completeness of evidence)

Stage 4: Recover systems, data, and connectivity

In this final stage, while responding to an incident, system is recovered to operate normally, authorize that the systems are functioning usually, and remediate vulnerabilities to prevent similar incidents from happening. Following are some key tasks during recovery:

- Restoring backups / restoring modified files from backups
- Reconnecting networks; rebuilding systems; and restoring, recreating, or correcting information.

- Restoring registry changes
- Resetting passwords of compromised accounts
- Installing patches, Hotfixes

It is significant to make sure that systems are operating normally again and are now secured from being re-compromised, which can often be achieved by carrying out an independent penetration test of the affected systems.

Attackers will try to get back into the network through all the approaches at their disposal. They will also come back knowing that they are being investigated and that their existing tactics, techniques, and procedures have been discovered. Therefore, it is significant to confirm that all elements of the attack have been eradicated and that the attackers cannot carry out further attacks.

When systems have been recovered and controls have been tested, stakeholders must then be provided with a summary of what took place. The team must report that eradication was completed successfully and note any exceptions and other significant findings. Briefings to stakeholders about the results must be well planned and conducted soon after the incident.

Phase 3: Follow Up

There are some follow-up actions needed after an incident is responded to. This follow-up task not only helps the incident responders to summarize what happen, but also helps to report the entire incident to relevant stakeholders. At last, this follow-up task also helps security teams to take necessary actions to avoid such attacks in future.

Stage 1: Investigate the incident more thoroughly

Thoroughly summarizing the incident will benefit you to find out what actually occurred, improvements required at security controls, and how to prevent the incident from recurring.

As part of this investigation, you must consider:

1. Carrying out Root Cause Analysis (RCA)

- The Five-Whys approach
- Why-Because Analysis (WBA)
- Cause-and Effect (fishbone) diagrams

1. Measuring the Business Impact Analysis of the incident

You must carry out enough investigation to find the perpetrators of the incident, which may include a specialist support, such as from forensic investigators.

Stage 2: Report the incident to relevant stakeholders

When an incident has been handled, formal reporting will often be compulsory to both internal and external stakeholders. Key questions to consider include:

- What are our reporting requirements?
- Who do I report to?
- What do I report?
- In what format do I report?
- What is the objective of reporting?

After you have answered these questions, the actual reporting itself must include:

- A full explanation of the nature of the incident, its history, and what actions were taken to recover from it
- A realistic estimate of the financial cost of the incident, and other impacts on the business, such as in terms of damage to reputation, loss of management control or impaired growth
- Recommendations regarding improved or additional controls required to prevent, detect, remediate, or recover from incidents more successfully.

Stage 3: Carry out a Post Incident Review

During a post incident review, important data about the incident must be discussed. Questions to be answered in such a review can contain:

1. How well did the staff and management perform in dealing with the incident? Were the documented procedures followed? Were they adequate?
2. What information was needed sooner?
3. Were any steps or actions taken that might have inhibited the recovery?
4. Could any unforeseen events have been prevented?
5. What would the staff and management do differently the next time a similar incident occurs?
6. How could information sharing with other organizations have been improved?
7. What corrective actions can prevent similar incidents in the future?
8. What precursors or indicators should be watched for in the future to detect similar incidents?
9. How can results be fed back into our risk assessment methodology?
10. What lessons have we learned?

To support an active post incident review, all key discussions and decisions conducted during the eradication event must be well documented. A report must be produced from the post incident review and presented to all applicable stakeholders.

Stage 4: Communicate and build on lessons learned

An important section of following up an incident is to document, communicate and build on lessons learned. This must be viewed as an on-going process through which you can cooperate and learn from previous mistakes, incidents, and experiences.

Communication to all stakeholders must be clear, concise, and focused on problem resolution and control improvement. It must clearly classify any gaps that remain and propose efforts to mitigate them.

An action plan must be created that clarifies how the organization will leverage lessons learned from the incident to develop more resilience in the face of future cyber security attacks. The action plan must contain projects or initiatives, technical and nontechnical, that will help decrease an attacker's chance of success and respond to an attacker's activities more quickly and effectively. Analysis of the incident must consider whether technical capability gaps contributed to the attacker's success or whether people or process gaps were the main culprit.

Each action must be assigned to a named individual and given an appropriate priority and completion date. The status of all action must then be monitored to certify that they are being completed in a timely and effective manner.

Stage 5: Update key information, controls, and documents

It is significant to update your incident response methods, controls, and related documents.

- Incident management methodologies
- Incident management preparatory activities
- Management controls (e.g., training and awareness)
- Technical controls (e.g., patching, configuring system logs, and use of intrusion prevention/detection tools)

- Business continuity or crisis management arrangements
- Internal IT auditing procedures

When updating controls, research open that the attack vectors producing most concern were:

- Poorly designed web applications
- Misconfigured systems
- Internet downloads
- Personal devices (e.g., tablet or smart phone)
- Authorized third parties (e.g., customers, suppliers, business partners).

Stage 6: Perform Trend Analysis

You must keep records about all security incidents, and their status along with other relevant information. You must review applicable incident data regularly to help:

- Evaluate patterns and trends of incidents
- Classify common factors that have influenced incidents
- Check the effectiveness of controls (e.g., which controls are better at preventing, detecting, and delaying incidents or minimizing their business impact)
- Understand the costs and impacts associated with incidents

Don't miss out!

Visit the website below and you can sign up to receive emails whenever Publicancy Ltd publishes a new book. There's no charge and no obligation.

https://books2read.com/r/B-A-PWNZ-MXULC

BOOKS 2 READ

Connecting independent readers to independent writers.

About the Author

Publicancy® is a publishing and marketing platform that unleashes the creative genius inside everyone. Publicancy makes it easy for authors to get their books designed, published, promoted, and sell professionally. Publicancy was founded in 2018 and includes a team of design; Internet and media veterans who share a passion for helping people bring their stories to life.

Read more at https://publicancy.com/.

Milton Keynes UK
Ingram Content Group UK Ltd.
UKHW052101241123
433194UK00014B/745